Also by Bill Watterson:

CALVIN AND HOBBES
SOMETHING UNDER THE BED IS DROOLING
YUKON HO!
WEIRDOS FROM ANOTHER PLANET
LAZY SUNDAY BOOK
REVENGE OF THE BABY-SAT
THE AUTHORITATIVE CALVIN AND HOBBES
SCIENTIFIC PROGRESS GOES 'BOINK'
ATTACK OF THE DERANGED MUTANT KILLER MONSTER SNOW GOONS

Taken from CALVIN AND HOBBES:
CALVIN AND HOBBES 1: THEREBY HANGS A TALE
CALVIN AND HOBBES 3: IN THE SHADOW OF THE NIGHT

Calvin and Hobbes

2: ONE DAY THE WIND WILL CHANGE

BILL WATTERSON

WARNER BOOKS

A *Warner* Book

First published in Great Britain in 1992
by Warner Books

The contents of this edition were first published as part
of *Calvin and Hobbes* © 1987 by Bill Watterson, published by
Sphere Books 1988

ISBN 0 7474 1159 X

Printed and bound in Great Britain by
Cox & Wyman Ltd, Reading

Warner Books
A Division of
Little, Brown and Company (UK) Limited
165 Great Dover Street
London SE1 4YA

TO MELISSA

LEAVE YOUR TIGER IN THE CAR, CALVIN.
CAN'T HOBBES COME ALONG, DAD? HE WON'T EAT ANYBODY!
NO, CALVIN. LET'S GO.
WELL, AT LEAST LET ME OPEN THE WINDOW AND GIVE HIM SOME AIR.
SEE IF HE'LL LEAVE THE KEYS, TOO, SO I CAN LISTEN TO THE RADIO.

CALVIN, YOUR MOTHER AND I HAVE DECIDED TO GIVE YOU AN ALLOWANCE.
IT'S IMPORTANT THAT ONE LEARNS THE VALUE OF MONEY.
MONEY! HA HA HA! I'M RICH! I'M RICH! I CAN BUY OFF ANYONE! THE WORLD IS MINE!
WATTERSON
POWER! FRIEND
PRESTIGE!
I BLEW IT AGAIN, DEAR!
I CAN BUY IT ALL! I'M FREE! HA HA HA HA!

WHEN I GROW UP, I WANT TO BE A RADICAL TERRORIST.
MM HMM..
I'M GOING TO INHALE THIS CAN OF PESTICIDE.
MM HMM..
I'M GOING TO WATCH TV ALL NIGHT.
THAT'S WHAT *YOU* THINK, BUSTER!
YOU CAN NEVER TELL IF THEY'RE LISTENING OR NOT.
WATTERSON

HERE'S A GOOD MOVIE! "VAMPIRE SORORITY BABES"!
IT SAYS YOU HAVE TO BE EIGHTEEN TO GET IN.
HECK, THAT'S NO PROBLEM! LET'S GO!
THIS IS A NEW ONE.
TWO PLEASE. ...I MEAN, ONE.
WATERSON

I THINK IT'S TIME WE HAD A NEW DAD AROUND HERE. WHEN DOES YOUR TERM OF OFFICE EXPIRE?
SORRY, CALVIN, I WAS APPOINTED DAD FOR LIFE.
FOR LIFE?! WHAT ABOUT A RECALL VOTE? WHAT ABOUT IMPEACHMENT?
THERE ARE NO PROVISIONS FOR EITHER.
DID YOU WRITE THIS CONSTITUTION YOURSELF, OR WHAT?
WELL, YOUR MOM HELPED SOME, TOO.
WATTERSON

AACHOO!
GESUNDHEIT!
OKAY! HOW MANY MONSTERS ARE UNDER MY BED TONIGHT?

JUST ONE.
THAT'S GOOD, HOBBES! WE OUTNUMBER HIM!
HEE HEE! WANNA *GET* HIM?
YEAH! SEE IF YOU CAN REACH THE BASEBALL BAT! HEH HEH!

QUIT SHOVING, YOU HOGS!
WATTERSON
MOMMMMM!
NICE GOING, MAURICE.

You're gonna taste asphalt fifth period, Twinky. Just so you know.
GREAT. I'M DEAD.
FIFTH PERIOD - "STUDIES IN CONTEMPORARY STATE-SPONSORED TERRORISM."
... ALSO KNOWN AS GYM CLASS.
WATERSON

I CAN'T GET A BABY SITTER ANYWHERE! WHAT SHOULD WE DO?
WE WON'T BE GONE LONG. COULDN'T CALVIN BE LEFT FOR A COUPLE HOURS UNSUPERVISED?
HA HA HA HA HA
HO HO HO HEE HE
HA
HOO HO
HO
HAR
HA
HEE HEE
...SERIOUSLY... WHAT SHOULD WE DO?
WATTERSON

OKAY, CALVIN. WE'LL BE BACK IN A COUPLE OF HOURS.
YOU AND HOBBES JUST WATCH TV AND BE GOOD, OKAY?
DID YOU HEAR THAT? WE GET TO WATCH TV!!
HOORAY!
VIDEORAMA? I'D LIKE TO RENT A VCR AND SOME MOVIES!
ASK IF THEY HAVE "ATTACK OF THE COED CANNIBALS."

WELL, THE HOUSE IS STILL STANDING. CALVIN MUST HAVE GONE TO BED.
HIS LIGHT IS STILL ON. ...CALVIN? ARE YOU AWAKE?
EEP!
DID YOU WATCH A SCARY MOVIE ?!?
NO. DON'T COME IN. THE RUG IS RIGGED TOO.
WATTERSON

WHAP!
SMASH
TINKLE
DING
SHATTER
CLINK
WOW. FIRST TRY!
WATERSON

WATERSON
DOWNTOWN TOKYO!
AARRGHHGH
GODZILLA.

HOW CAN I GET SOME MONEY?
...SHORT OF EARNING IT, I MEAN...
I WANT A GRENADE LAUNCHER, MOM. WHEN'S CHRISTMAS?
NOT FOR A LONG TIME.
WHEN'S MY BIRTHDAY?
NOT FOR A LONG TIME.

WHEN'S MY ALLOWANCE?
YOU SPENT IT ALREADY.
DO I HAVE ANY STOCKS I CAN CASH? WAR BONDS?!?
CALVIN, I'M TRYING TO WORK!
CAN I BORROW SOME SOAP?
YES, YOU CAN BORROW SOME SOAP. HAVE ALL THE SOAP YOU WANT.
4 SaLE ChEEP!
WATTERSON

BOY, IS IT COLD!
YOU SHOULD GET A GOOD FUR COAT LIKE MINE.
WOOF! WHAT DID YOU EAT FOR BREAKFAST? CEMENT?
LOOK, WAS THIS *MY* IDEA?
WATTERSON

OH NO, I LOST MY QUARTER!
WHERE DID YOU LOSE IT?
IT'S SOMEWHERE IN THIS FIELD.
WE'LL NEVER FIND IT. YOU'LL HAVE TO WAIT TILL THE SNOW MELTS.
TILL THE SNOW MELTS? IT'S 25 CENTS!!
WATERSON
ZZZZZZZ

WANNA SEE SOMETHING WEIRD?
WATCH. YOU PUT BREAD IN THIS SLOT AND PUSH DOWN THIS LEVER...
THEN IN A FEW MINUTES, TOAST POPS UP!
DING!
WOW. WHERE DOES THE BREAD GO?
BEATS ME. ISN'T THAT WEIRD?
WATTERSON

TOO BAD THE WORLD WILL BE ENDING SOON.
BEG YOUR PARDON?
HALLEY'S COMET. COMETS ARE HARBINGERS OF DOOM.
WATERSON
NO, THEY AREN'T. THAT'S JUST SUPERSTITION.
REALLY??
GUESS I'D BETTER WRITE THAT BOOK REPORT.

HOW ARE YOU TODAY?
FINE.
I WANT THE TOP OF MY HEAD SHAVED, AND THE SIDES DYED PINK AND CUT IN HORIZONTAL STRIPES, OK?
MA'AM?
GIVE HIM THE USUAL, PETE.
WATTERSON
WELL I GUESS THIS GUY KNOWS WHICH SIDE HIS BREAD IS BUTTERED ON!

THERE, HOW'S THAT LOOK?
THAT'S GREAT. PERFECT.
WITHOUT QUESTION, THIS IS THE FINEST HAIRCUT I HAVE EVER RECEIVED.
NEVER CRITICIZE A GUY WITH A RAZOR...
WATTERSON

READY?
LET ME CHECK WHAT THE DEDUCTIBLE IS ON MY INSURANCE POLICY...
MUNCH MUNCH
WOULD YOU CARE FOR A SOFT DRINK?
OK.

H-H-HERE Y-YOU A-A-ARE!
BONK!
BONK!
ANY DESSERT?
NO, THANKS.
WE'LL BE LANDING SHORTLY.
THE CAPTAIN HAS TURNED OFF THE SEAT BELT SIGN. THANK YOU FOR CHOOSING CALVIN'S FLIGHT 240 NON-STOP TO STONEY GULCH.
NEXT TIME I WON'T TAKE THE DINNER FLIGHT.
WATERSON

DO YOU LOVE ME, DAD?
OF COURSE I DO, CALVIN.
WATERSON
WOULD YOU STILL LOVE ME IF I DID SOMETHING BAD?
WELL OF COURSE ... I ... WOULD...
I MEAN SOMETHING REALLY REALLY..
CALVIN, WHAT DID YOU DO?!

WELL, DAD, YOUR POLLS ARE REAL HIGH THIS WEEK.
I'M GLAD TO HEAR THAT.
YEP, THOSE POLLED THINK YOU'RE DOING A FINE JOB AS DAD.
IN FACT, WITH A LITTLE PUSH TODAY, YOUR POLITICAL STOCK COULD REACH A RECORD HIGH.
NICE TRY. GO HELP YOUR MOM WITH THE DISHES.
OOH DAD! SUICIDE! OOH! OOH!
WATTERSON

HERE COMES MOE, THE CLASS BULLY.
HE'S NOT SMART, BUT HE'S STREETWISE.
THAT MEANS HE KNOWS WHAT STREET HE LIVES ON.
WATTERSON

TOLL BOOTH, DAD! YOU CAN'T PUT THE CAR IN UNTIL YOU PAY ME A QUARTER!
WHY SHOULD I PAY YOU TO PUT *MY* CAR IN *MY* GARAGE?
BECAUSE IF YOU DON'T, I'LL PULL THE DOOR DOWN ON THE HOOD AS YOU DRIVE IN!
WHAT A CHEAPSKATE.
WATTERSON

A LITTLE LOWER...OK, FINE!
THANKS FOR HELPING ME PUT UP THIS SWING.
WATTERSON

WHERE DID YOU EVER FIND THIS GREAT TIRE?

CALVIN! I'VE GOT TO GO TO WORK!!

WHAT'S THAT CEREAL YOU'RE EATING?
MILK
IT'S MY NEW FAVORITE, "CHOCOLATE FROSTED SUGAR BOMBS."
HAVE A TASTE.
THANK YOU.
MFFPBTH!! S-SW-SW SWEET!!
ACTUALLY, THEY'RE KINDA BLAND TILL YOU SCOOP SUGAR ON 'EM.

HOW COME WE PLAY WAR AND NOT PEACE?
TOO FEW ROLE MODELS.
I'LL BE THE FEARLESS AMERICAN DEFENDER OF LIBERTY AND DEMOCRACY..
... AND YOU CAN BE THE LOATHSOME GODLESS COMMUNIST OPPRESSOR.

WE'RE AT WAR, SO IF YOU GET HIT WITH A DART, YOU'RE DEAD AND THE OTHER SIDE WINS, OK?
GOTCHA.
GO!
WAP
WAP
KIND OF A STUPID GAME, ISN'T IT?

CAN I BE EXCUSED?
NOT UNTIL YOU FINISH YOUR SALMON.
BLAUGHHH!
WATERSON
CAN I EAT IT UPSTAIRS WHILE I DO MY HOMEWORK?
WELL, I SUPPOSE.
I BROUGHT YOU YOUR FAVORITE! HOW'S IT COMING?
WELL, I COULDN'T FIGURE OUT THIS SUBTRACTION PROBLEM, SO I PUT "ATLANTA, GEORGIA"...

HEY, SUSIE, WANNA SEE A MAGIC TRICK?
FIRST, I'LL NEED AN ORDINARY QUARTER...
!
NOW I'LL DISAPPEAR! HA HA HA!
HEY! DIDN'T I SAY IT WAS A TRICK??
WATERSON

LOOK! A DECODER RING!
WOW! WE CAN SEND EACH OTHER SECRET MESSAGES IN CODE!
HA HA! NOW MOM AND DAD WON'T BE ABLE TO UNDERSTAND US AT ALL!
...NOT THAT THEY DO ANYWAY...

RISE AND SHINE, CALVIN!
MFGPBTHBBPT
THE EARLY BIRD GETS THE WORM!
BIG INCENTIVE.
WATERSON

I'VE DECIDED WE SHOULD BE "COOLER" THAN WE ARE.
WE'RE NOT COOL?
SURE WE'RE COOL. BUT WE'RE NOT AS COOL AS WE **COULD** BE.
COOL PEOPLE WEAR DARK GLASSES!
IT'S COOL TO BUMP INTO THINGS?
YOU DON'T MOVE, YOU JUST HANG AROUND.
WATERSON

HEY, DAD, WILL YOU BUY ME A FLAME THROWER?
OF COURSE NOT. DON'T BE SILLY.
EVEN IF I DIDN'T USE IT IN THE HOUSE?

DID YOU ASK YOUR MOM IF YOU COULD JUMP OFF THE ROOF?

QUESTIONS I KNOW THE ANSWERS TO I DON'T NEED TO ASK, RIGHT?

IS THIS BLANKET BIG ENOUGH?
PERFECT!

SEE, I'LL JUST GRAB ALL THE CORNERS AND MAKE A PARACHUTE!
YOU CAN WATCH AS I FLOAT TO THE GROUND, GENTLY AS A LEAF!
GERONIMO!!

CRUNCH
HIS MOM'S GOING TO HAVE A FIT ABOUT THOSE ROSE BUSHES.
WATTERSON

I TOLD YOU I'M NOT SICK! WHAT'S THAT? WILL IT HURT?
IT'S A TONGUE DEPRESSOR. IT WON'T HURT AT ALL.
WHAT'S *THAT*? WILL IT HURT?
IT'S A STETHOSCOPE. IT WON'T HURT AT ALL.
WHAT'S *THAT*? WILL IT HURT?
IT'S A CATTLE PROD. IT HURTS A LITTLE LESS THAN A BRANDING IRON.
LITTLE KIDS HAVE NO SENSE OF HUMOR.
WATTERSON

HEY, DOC, WHY ARE YOU RUBBING MY ARM WITH COTTON? ARE YOU GOING TO PUT A LEECH THERE?
ARE YOU GOING TO BLEED ME? YOU'RE NOT GOING TO AMPUTATE, ARE YOU? ARE YOU??
WHAT'S THAT? IS THAT A SHOT? ARE YOU GOING TO... AAUGHH! IT WENT CLEAR THROUGH MY ARM!! OW OW OW OW!!!
I'M DYING! I HOPE YOU'VE PAID YOUR MALPRACTICE INSURANCE, YOU QUACK!! WHERE'S MY MOM???
WATTERSON

"SAFARI AL" HACKS HIS WAY THROUGH THE JUNGLE!
SUDDENLY, A GIANT GORILLA RIPS THROUGH THE FOLIAGE!
CLEAN YOUR ROOM.
WATTERSON
WHAT?
YOU HEARD ME. IT'S A JUNGLE IN HERE!

SEEN ANY UFOs YET?
NOPE.
KEEP WATCHING THE MOON. ALIENS USUALLY TRY TO SNEAK UP FROM BEHIND IT.
WHAT ARE YOU DOING OUT HERE IN YOUR PAJAMAS? GET BACK IN BED!!
MOTHERS, ON THE OTHER HAND, SNEAK UP FROM BEHIND THE PACHYSANDRA PATCH.
WATTERSON

GOOD NIGHT, HOBBES.
GOOD NIGHT.
DO YOU BELIEVE IN GHOSTS?
WATTERSON

WHAT DO YOU HAVE FOR LUNCH, SUSIE? MAYBE I'LL TRADE YOU.
UGH! A CROSS SECTION OF A DACHSHUND. NO, THANKS.
IT'S BOLOGNA!
I WONDER WHAT I HAVE FOR LUNCH TODAY.
IT'S LUNCH TIME! HA HA HA! I THINK I'LL HAVE THIS LITTLE KID!!

HELP! I'M BEING EATEN ALIVE BY MY OWN LUNCH! SOMEBODY GET ME A FORK!
HE'S GOT ME!!
AAARRRGGHH
WHAM
WHAM
WHAM
WHAM
HA! I KILLED IT WITH MY THERMOS! SEE? IT'S BLEEDING JELLY!
NO WONDER THIS SEAT WASN'T TAKEN.
WATTERSON

SOMEWHERE IN COMMUNIST RUSSIA I'LL BET THERE'S A LITTLE BOY WHO HAS NEVER KNOWN ANYTHING BUT **CENSORSHIP** AND **OPPRESSION**.
BUT MAYBE HE'S HEARD ABOUT **AMERICA**, AND HE DREAMS OF LIVING IN THIS LAND OF **FREEDOM** AND OPPORTUNITY!
SOMEDAY, I'D LIKE TO MEET THAT LITTLE BOY...
...AND TELL HIM THE AWFUL **TRUTH** ABOUT THIS PLACE!!
CALVIN, BE QUIET AND EAT THE STUPID LIMA BEANS.

SPACEMAN SPIFF, BOLD INTERPLANETARY EXPLORER, SPIES A ZARG!
SPIFF CALIBRATES HIS BLASTER. READY...AIM...
CALVIN, IF YOU SHOOT THAT PAPER CLIP AT ME, I'LL GET YOUR BOTTOM HAULED TO THE PRINCIPAL'S OFFICE SO FAST YOU'LL THINK YOU WERE IN A **TIME WARP!!**
CONFOUND IT. THE BLASTER JAMMED.
WATTERSON

IT LOOKS LIKE HOBBES BURST A SEAM HERE. I'LL GET MY SEWING KIT.
IT'S JUST A LITTLE CUT. I DON'T NEED AN OPERATION. THIS IS UNNECESSARY SURGERY!
IT'S NOT SURGERY. YOU'RE JUST GETTING A COUPLE STITCHES! WHAT'S THE BIG DEAL?
YOUR MOM NEVER USES ANY ANESTHETIC.
WATERSON

WHAT A PECULIAR DREAM I HAD LAST NIGHT!
I DREAMED I WAS IN A BIG FIGHT WITH A FEROCIOUS WEASEL!
WHAT DO YOU SUPPOSE IT MEANS?
WATTERSON
IT MEANS YOU'RE SLEEPING ON THE FLOOR TONIGHT, YOU NINCOMPOOP!

HEY DAD, REMEMBER OUR CAR?
WHY SURE.
WAIT A MINUTE. WHAT DO YOU MEAN, "REMEMBER"?
HOBBES, I HAVE A CONJECTURAL MORAL QUESTION. MAYBE YOU CAN HELP.
SURE.
SUPPOSE I DID SOMETHING BAD. SHOULD I TELL DAD?
HOW BAD ARE WE SUPPOSING?

WELL, HYPOTHETICALLY, LET'S SAY PRETTY BAD. LIKE TO HIS CAR, HYPOTHETICALLY.
HOW BAD, HYPOTHETICALLY, TO HIS CAR?
SHOULD WE PRETEND IT COULD BE FIXED?
WELL, LET'S PRETEND IT WAS **REAL** BAD.
IF WE IMAGINED HE COULD **FIND** THE CAR, WE COULD PRETEND IT MIGHT BE FIXED.
I SEE.
YOU CAN KEEP THE BOOK. I'LL CALL THE BUS STATION.
"¿QUE PASA, SEÑORITA? ¡I AM EL FUGITIVO!"
WATERSON

WHY CAN'T I STAY UP LATE? YOU GUYS CAN!
IT'S NOT FAIR!
THE WORLD ISN'T FAIR, CALVIN.
I KNOW, BUT WHY ISN'T IT EVER UNFAIR IN MY FAVOR?
WATTERSON

THE VALIANT SPACEMAN SPIFF IS BEING PURSUED BY A DISGUSTING SCUM BEING!
SPIFF SPOTS HIS HOVERING SPACESHIP AND BOLTS FOR THE LADDER!
BUT HE'S TOO LATE! THE AWFUL SCUM BEING IS UPON HIM! IT'S ALL OVER!
IT'S ALL OVER!!
I TOLD YOU THREE TIMES RECESS WAS OVER! NOW GET INSIDE!
WATTERSON

AS DICTATOR, I HAVE THE SOLE VOICE IN GOVERNMENT!
I WILL NOT TOLERATE DISSENT!
I ALONE SHALL DECIDE THE GOOD! I ALONE SHALL..
TIME FOR BED, CALVIN.
COULDN'T WE VOTE ON THIS?
WATERSON

IF YOU COULD WISH FOR ANYTHING, WHAT WOULD IT BE?
A BIG SUNNY FIELD TO BE IN.
A STUPID FIELD?! YOU'VE GOT THAT NOW! THINK BIG! RICHES! POWER! PRETEND YOU COULD HAVE ANYTHING!
ACTUALLY, IT'S HARD TO ARGUE WITH SOMEONE WHO LOOKS SO HAPPY.
Z

HERE FISH!
THEY MUST KNOW THAT ONE.

AAGHH!
CHOMP!
ARE THE FISH BITING?
DROP DEAD, HOBBES.
WATERSON

OOPS! I FORGOT TO READ CHAPTER FIVE FOR SCHOOL TOMORROW.
WHAT ARE YO
GOING TO DO
CATCH A QUICK COLD.
COUGH COUGH
YOU SOUND TERRIBLE, CALVIN. I'LL GET YOU SOME COUGH MEDICINE.
IT WASN'T ME COUGHING. IT WAS HOBBES.

ME? IT WASN'T ME!
I KNOW. BUT THAT COUGH SYRUP TASTES AWFUL.
SO YOU'RE GOING TO HAVE *ME* TAKE IT? NOTHING DOING, BUSTER. I REFUSE!
HERE YOU GO, CALVIN. OPEN UP.
NOT ME! GIVE IT TO HOBBES! HE'S THE ONE WHO..
GLOOMP

ACKTHP!
PBTHBBPPTH!!
HACK
HACK

MMMM! THAT COUGH MEDICINE IS GOOD! YOU SHOULD TRY SOME! REALLY!
YOU'RE NOT FOOLING ME ONE BIT, YOU STINKER.

I CAN'T GET THIS MODEL AIRPLANE TO LOOK RIGHT.
THESE DIRECTIONS ARE IMPOSSIBLE!
RRRRRGGGHHHHH
WHAM
WHAM
WHAM
HIT BY ANTI-AIRCRAFT GUNS.
YOUR PLANES DO SEEM TO RUN INTO THOSE, DON'T THEY?
WATTERSON

TOMMY TOLD A FUNNY STORY AT SCHOOL TODAY. I ALMOST DIED!
TELL IT TO ME.
WELL, ACTUALLY THE STORY ITSELF WASN'T SO FUNNY...
...IT WAS THE WAY HE TOLD IT.
HOW DID HE TELL IT?
HE WAS DRINKING MILK AND WHEN HE LAUGHED, IT CAME UP HIS NOSE!
WATTERSON

You've got two periods to live, Twinky.
Then it's gym class, and I turn you into hamburger casserole!
I HATE GYM CLASS.
COACH THINKS VIOLENCE IS AEROBIC.
WATTERSON

WHERE'S MY JACKET?
I'VE LOOKED EVERYWHERE! UNDER THE BED, OVER MY CHAIR...
...ON THE STAIRS, ON THE HALL FLOOR, IN THE KITCHEN... IT'S JUST NOT ANYWHERE!
OH, HERE IT IS! WHO PUT IT IN THE STUPID CLOSET?!?
WATTERSON

HOCUS-POCUS, ABRACADABRA!
I COMMAND MY HOMEWORK TO DO ITSELF! **HOMEWORK, BE DONE!**
WATERSON
FLIP FLIP FLIP
RATS.

DO YOU EVER THINK ABOUT THE END OF THE WORLD AS WE KNOW IT?
YOU MEAN A NUCLEAR WAR?
I THINK MOM WAS REFERRING TO IF SHE EVER CATCHES ME LETTING THE AIR OUT OF THE CAR TIRES AGAIN.

I'M TAKING THE UMBRELLA OUTSIDE.
WELL, THAT'S SHOWING A LITTLE FORESIGHT FOR ONCE. GOOD FOR YOU.
WAIT A MINUTE...
YOU REALLY THINK THIS WILL WORK?
OF COURSE! LET'S GO!

SMASH!
BONK
BONK
BONK

ITY BIPPITY BIPPITY BIPPITY

LOOK! I'M FLYING!!
WATTERSON

I HAD MY EYES SHUT. HOW WAS IT?
GREAT! WHAT A RIDE! LET'S GET SOME OTHER KIDS AND CHARGE 'EM!

FEARLESS SPACEMAN SPIFF CLOSES IN ON THE FLEEING ZARGONS!
ONCE AGAIN OUR HERO IS ABOUT TO TEACH VICIOUS ALIEN SCUM THAT VIRTUE IS ITS OWN REWARD! HE LOCKS ONTO TARGET!
PSST, CALVIN! WHAT WAS THE CAPITAL OF POLAND UNTIL 1600?
KRAKOW.
THANKS.
KRAKOW! KRAKOW! TWO DIRECT HITS!
WATTERSON

THE TYRANNOSAURUS LUMBERS ACROSS THE PREHISTORIC VALLEY...
THE TERRIFYING LIZARD IS THREE STORIES TALL AND HIS MOUTH IS FILLED WITH SIX-INCH CHISELS OF DEATH!
WITH A FEW MIGHTY STEPS, THE DINOSAUR IS UPON A TRIBE OF FLEEING CAVEMEN. HE DEVOURS THEM ONE BY ONE!
AARRGH! AAIEEE! AAUGHH!
CALVIN, EAT YOUR POPCORN QUIETLY!
WATTERSON

WHICH ONE?
THAT LONG ONE.
WHAT DOES THIS WORD MEAN?
!
I DON'T KNOW.
YOU DO TOO!! ALL RIGHT! WHERE'S A DICTIONARY??
WATERSON

CAN I WATCH THE MOVIE "KILLER PROM QUEEN" ON TV?
NO.
DO I HAVE TO EAT THIS SLIMY ASPARAGUS?
YES.
CAN I STAY UP TILL MIDNIGHT?
NO.
THERE'S AN INVERSE RELATIONSHIP BETWEEN HOW GOOD SOMETHING IS FOR YOU, AND HOW MUCH FUN IT IS.

LET'S SEE WHAT HAPPENS IF YOU COOK POPCORN WITHOUT A LID.
POW
KAPWING
POW
BANG
ZANG
BOING
HECK, THAT'S MORE FUN THAN EXPLODING A POTATO IN THE MICROWAVE!
LET'S DO SOME MORE!
WATTERSON

C'MON, CALVIN. WE'RE GOING TO THE STORE.
CAN HOBBES COME?
NO, JUST LEAVE HIM HERE.
BUT I WANT HIM TO COME WITH US!!
IF YOU CAN'T WIN BY REASON, GO FOR VOLUME.

HONEY, WE HAVE TO LEAVE SOON. IS CALVIN TAKING HIS BATH?
OH GOOD.
WHILE I'M TAKING MY BATH, YOU CAN BRUSH YOUR TEETH AND COMB YOUR HAIR.
RIGHT.

YOUR DAD WON'T MIND IF I USE HIS COLOGNE, WILL HE?
WELL, GO EASY THIS TIME.
THINK I SHOULD SHAVE?
NO, GO FOR THE DON JOHNSON FUZZY LOOK.
HERE'S A TIE AND ONE OF MY SPORT COATS.

PERFECT! RIGHT OUT OF "GQ"!
BOY, I LOOK GOOD IN ANYTHING, DON'T I?

REFRESH MY MEMORY. *HOW* DID I GET TALKED INTO THIS ONE?
MY FRIEND WOULD LIKE TO SEE THE WINE LIST.
WATTERSON

SO THE CONTRACTOR SAYS IT WILL COST ABOUT $200 TO FIX.
OH, THAT DUMB KID!
WELL, IT'S ALL PART OF RAISING A CHILD, RIGHT?
MM.
WATTERSON

YOU'RE NOT SORRY WE HAD CALVIN, ARE YOU?
ARE YOU?
I ASKED FIRST.... BESIDES, IT WASN'T ALL MY DECISION.
ALL I KNOW IS THAT I OFFERED TO BUY US A DACHSHUND, BUT NO, YOU SAID...

DO YOU THINK THERE'S A GOD?
WELL SOMEBODY'S OUT TO GET ME.
WATTERSON

SPACEMAN SPIFF CLOSES IN ON THE ALIEN VESSEL!
THE ALIEN, BEING UNNATURALLY STUPID, IS BLISSFULLY IGNORANT OF ITS IMMINENT DOOM!
OUR HERO LOCKS ONTO TARGET AND WARMS UP HIS FRAP-RAY BLASTER!
MISS WORMWOOD!!
ZOUNDS! A GORKON DEATH STATION APPEARS! EVASIVE ACTION!
WATTERSON

WHACK!
WOW! ANOTHER HOLE IN ONE!

WOW! THREE NEW MAGAZINES FOR ME TODAY.
YESTERDAY I GOT FIVE. I LOVE GETTING ALL THIS MAIL.
HOW COME YOU RECEIVE ALL THESE MAGAZINES?
WATTERSON
I WENT TO THE LIBRARY AND FILLED OUT ALL THE SUBSCRIPTION CARDS THAT SAID "BILL ME LATER."

I LOVE SATURDAY MORNING CARTOONS.
WHAT CLASSIC HUMOR!
THIS IS WHAT ENTERTAINMENT IS ALL ABOUT.
...IDIOTS, EXPLOSIVES, AND FALLING ANVILS.
WATERSON

WANNA GO CATCH SOME FISH?
SURE.
UGH. I DON'T WANT TO TOUCH THESE WORMS. WILL YOU PUT ONE ON MY HOOK?
ME? I'M NOT GONNA SPEAR ANY WORMS!

I KNOW... LET'S JUST DUMP THE WORMS IN THE WATER, AND WHEN THE FISH COME UP TO EAT THEM, WE'LL CATCH THEM IN THE NET!
PRETTY SMART, HUH? THAT'S WHAT I LIKE ABOUT SURVIVING IN THE WILD – PITTING OUR WITS AGAINST THE RAGING ELEMENTS!
THE WORMS ARE GETTING SOGGY.
OOH, THEY'RE STARTING TO SINK.

BLIP
BLOOP
BLORP

LET'S PIT OUR WITS AGAINST SOME FAST FOOD CHEESEBURGERS. THOSE COME IN NEAT LITTLE BOXES.
YEAH, WHO'D WANT TO EAT SOMETHING THAT EATS WORMS ANYWAY?
WATTERSON

CALVIN, THE HUMAN INSECT, WALKS ACROSS THE DINNER TABLE.
WITH PROPORTIONAL INSECT STRENGTH, HE PLACES A GIANT PEA ON THE EDGE OF A SPOON.
HE THEN CLIMBS TO THE TOP OF THE OTHER END...
...AND WITH A TINY JUMP...
CALVIN, STOP THAT!
WATERSON

IN HIS MINUSCULE SIZE, IT TAKES CALVIN, THE HUMAN INSECT, TEN MINUTES TO WALK ACROSS A BOOK'S PAGE!
AT THE OTHER END, HE SLOWLY LIFTS THE GIGANTIC SHEET!
THEN IT'S ANOTHER TEN-MINUTE JOURNEY BACK, AS HE TURNS IT OVER!
GEE, THE KID'S BEEN QUIET FOR ALMOST TWENTY MINUTES.
HE'S DOING HIS HOMEWORK.
WATTERSON

HERE'S A MOVIE WE SHOULD WATCH.
WHO'S IN IT?
IT SAYS, "JAPANESE CAST."
WATERSON
"TWO BIG RUBBERY MONSTERS SLUG IT OUT OVER MAJOR METROPOLITAN CENTERS IN A BATTLE FOR WORLD SUPREMACY."
DOESN'T THAT SOUND GREAT?
AND PEOPLE SAY THAT FOREIGN FILM IS INACCESSIBLE.

OH, ROSALYN, YOU'RE HERE! GOOD, COME IN!
WE REALLY APPRECIATE YOUR COMING ON SUCH SHORT NOTICE. WE'VE HAD A TERRIBLE TIME GETTING A BABY SITTER FOR TONIGHT.
HA HA. MAYBE LITTLE CALVIN HERE HAS GOTTEN HIMSELF A REPUTATION.
HA HA. YOU HAVE THE HALF UP FRONT?
YES, LET ME GET MY PURSE...
WATTERSON

HI, BABY DOLL, IT'S ME. YEAH, I'M BABY SITTING THE KID DOWN THE STREET.
YEAH, THAT'S RIGHT, THE LITTLE MONSTER. ... HMM?... WELL SO FAR, NO PROBLEM.
WATTERSON
HE HASN'T BEEN ANY TROUBLE. YOU JUST HAVE TO SHOW THESE KIDS WHO'S THE BOSS. ..MM HMM..
HOW MUCH LONGER TILL SHE LETS US OUT OF THE GARAGE?
SHE SAID 8 O'CLOCK, AND IT'S ALMOST 6:30 NOW...

THANKS AGAIN FOR BABY SITTING, ROSALYN.
CALVIN WAS NO TROUBLE AT ALL.
THAT'S GOOD. I'LL GET THE CAR AND DRIVE YOU HOME.
THERE YOU GO. GOOD NIGHT.
THANK YOU. GOOD NIGHT.
IS SHE GONE?
WATTERSON

WE'VE GOT A BABY SITTER TONIGHT.

READY?
READY.

CALVIN, THE BABY SITTER IS HERE! WE'RE GOING! BE GOOD, OK?

HI THERE. YOU MUST BE CALVIN.
HMMPH.
YOU'RE NOT MY MOM, SO I DON'T HAVE TO DO ANYTHING YOU SAY. I'M GOING TO DO WHATEVER I FEEL LIKE, SO JUST STAY OUT OF THE WAY.
CALVIN, TAKE A LOOK BY THE TELEPHONE AND TELL ME WHAT YOU SEE.

A NOTE MOM LEFT WITH EMERGENCY NUMBERS.
RIGHT. NOW YOU WOULDN'T WANT ME TO HAVE TO *CALL* ANY OF THOSE NUMBERS, WOULD YOU?
WELL, IT MUST BE 6:30. GUESS I'LL TURN IN.
FOR EIGHT BUCKS A NIGHT, I DON'T PUT UP WITH MUCH.
WATERSON

WHAT A GREAT NIGHT TO CAMP OUT!
WHERE'S OUR TENT? I THOUGHT THE SCOUTMASTER SAID TO SET THEM UP.
UH OH.
WHEN HE SAID TO PITCH THE TENT, I THREW IT AWAY.

THE BEST PART ABOUT THESE HIKES IS GETTING TO SEE SO MUCH WILDLIFE.
LOOK! A TIGER!
A TIGER?!
DON'T DO THAT!
WATERSON

WE'RE SEPARATED FROM THE TROOP AND HOPELESSLY LOST!
LEFT ALONE IN THE UNCOMPROMISING WILD TO SURVIVE BY OUR WITS UNAIDED!
HEY, DUMMY! THE SCOUTMASTER SAYS TO GRAB YOUR STUPID STUFFED TIGER AND GET YOUR REAR IN GEAR!
WE'LL TRY TO LOSE 'EM AGAIN OVER THE NEXT HILL.
WATERSON

GRAB THE HOTDOGS AND COME ON!
THE TROOP'S COOKING DINNER OVER THE FIRE.
OH THAT'S JUST GREAT.
HERE WE'VE BEEN LUGGING THIS DUMB MICROWAVE AROUND FOR NOTHING.
WATTERSON

BOP
SPIKE!
OH OH, WE'D BETTER LEAVE!
IT LOOKS LIKE SOME BIG PEOPLE WANT TO PLAY TENNIS.

THE CROCODILE FLOATS TO THE TOP OF THE MURKY AMAZON...
COMPLETELY MOTIONLESS, HE APPEARS TO BE ONLY A HARMLESS LOG.
A HIPPOPOTAMUS APPROACHES AND ENSURES ITS INSTANT DEATH!
WATTERSON
CALVIN, WHAT ARE YOU DOING? ARE YOU ALL RIGHT?
CLOSER... CLOSER...

LOOK, IT SAYS YOU HAVE TO BE EIGHTEEN TO BUY CIGARETTES.
EIGHTEEN?!? BY THEN I'LL KNOW BETTER!
MOM, CAN I HAVE A CIGARETTE?
SURE, CALVIN. I THINK YOUR GRANDFATHER LEFT SOME HERE. JUST SMOKE OUTSIDE, OK?
WOW!

YOUR MOM LET YOU HAVE A CIGARETTE?
FOR A MOM, SOMETIMES SHE'S PRETTY COOL.
EEEEEEP
BLAAUGH!
GAG
HACK
COUGH

YOU'D THINK THIS WOULD BE AN EASY HABIT TO BREAK.
WHEEZE
ACK
WATTERSON

WELL NOW... DID WE LEARN A LITTLE LESSON TODAY?
GASP ..YES...

TRUSTING PARENTS CAN BE HAZARDOUS TO YOUR HEALTH.

MOM! MOM! A BIG DOG KNOCKED ME DOWN AND HE STOLE HOBBES!
I TRIED TO CATCH HIM, BUT I COULDN'T, AND NOW I'VE LOST MY BEST FRIEND!
WELL CALVIN, IF YOU WOULDN'T DRAG THAT TIGER EVERYWHERE, THINGS LIKE THIS WOULDN'T HAPPEN.
THERE'S NO PROBLEM SO AWFUL THAT YOU CAN'T ADD SOME GUILT TO IT AND MAKE IT EVEN WORSE!

I CAN'T SLEEP AT ALL. POOR HOBBES! I WONDER WHERE HE IS. I HOPE HE'S OK.
SNIFF.. WHAT DID I EVER DO TO DESERVE THIS?
WHATEVER IT WAS, I'M *SORRY* ALREADY!
WATTERSON

LOST: MY TIGER, "HOBBES"
MAYBE YOU SHOULD DESCRIBE HIM.
ON THE QUIET SIDE. SOMEWHAT PECULIAR. A GOOD COMPANION, IN A WEIRD SORT OF WAY.
I MEAN, WHAT DOES HE LOOK LIKE?
OH.
WATTERSON

WELL LOOK, SOMEBODY LEFT A STUFFED TIGER OUT IN THE FIELD. HOW STRANGE.
LOOKS LIKE A DOG'S BEEN CHEWING ON YOU, FELLA.
WELL, NOTHING A LITTLE TEA PARTY WITH SOME OTHER STUFFED ANIMALS WOULDN'T HELP. C'MON.
WATTERSON

HOBBES! HOBBES! WHERE ARE YOU?!?
HELLO, CALVIN. WOULD YOU LIKE TO JOIN MY TEA PARTY?
HECK NO. I'M TRYING TO FIND MY BEST FRIEND, WHO'S BEEN KIDNAPPED BY A DOG. LEAVE ME ALONE.
WELL I THINK MR. CALVIN IS VERY RUDE, DON'T YOU, MR. TIGER? YES, I THINK SO TOO. MORE TEA, ANYONE?
WATTERSON

HEY, I SHOULD TELL SUSIE TO KEEP HER EYES OPEN FOR HOBBES.
SUSIE, I...
HOBBES!
YOU FOUND HOBBES! THANK YOU THANK YOU THANKYOUTHANKYOUTHANKYOUTHANKYOUTHANKYOUTHA
WELL! WASN'T MR. CALVIN A GENTLEMAN! I DO HOPE... HEY! WHO TOOK ALL THE COOKIES?!?

WHAT'S THAT SMELL?
EITHER MOM'S COOKING DINNER, OR SOMEBODY GOT SICK IN THE FURNACE DUCT.
BOY, DOES IT STINK IN HERE! WHAT ARE YOU COOKING FOR DINNER?!
I'M STEWING SOME MONKEY HEADS.
WHATEVER IT IS, I'M NOT EATING IT.

MONKEY HEADS?
THEY'LL BE SOGGY ENOUGH TO EAT IN ABOUT TWENTY MINUTES.
REALLY?? WE'RE HAVING MONKEY HEADS? WE ARE NOT. ...ARE THOSE REALLY MONKEY HEADS?
I'VE NEVER HAD MONKEY HEADS BEFORE! I WONDER WHAT THEY'RE LIKE.
WOW! MONKEY HEADS!
MM...KINDA SQUISHY. OOH LOOK, IS THAT A NOSE? WHAT'S THIS? BRAINS? I DIDN'T THINK THEY'D BE SO RUBBERY...
WHAT? I THOUGHT THESE WERE STUFFED PEPPERS. HONEY, WHAT THE HECK IS THIS?? WHATEVER IT IS, I'M NOT EATING IT!

SUSIE, WANNA HEAR A SECRET?
SURE.
I THINK THE PRINCIPAL IS A SPACE ALIEN SPY.
HE'S TRYING TO CORRUPT OUR YOUNG INNOCENT MINDS SO WE'LL BE UNABLE TO RESIST WHEN HIS PEOPLE INVADE EARTH!
PROMISE NOT TO TELL ANYONE?
DON'T WORRY.
WATERSON